The Dagger
Between Her Teeth

Jennifer LoveGrove

MISFIT

ECW PRESS

Published by ECW PRESS
2120 Queen Street East, Suite 200, Toronto, Ontario, Canada M4E 1E2

NATIONAL LIBRARY OF CANADA CATALOGUING IN PUBLICATION DATA

LoveGrove, Jennifer
The dagger between her teeth

ISBN 1-55022-511-1

I. Title.

PS8573.O8753D33 2002   C811'.6   C2001-904073-3
PR9199.4.I694D33 2002

Editor: Michael Holmes, a misFit book
Cover and Text design: Darren Holmes
Typesetting: Mary Bowness
Printing: AGMV / MARQUIS
Author photo: Kate Sutherland
Front cover photo: Geraint Cunnick, Photonica

This book is set in Goudy and Futura

The publication of *The Dagger Between Her Teeth* has been generously supported by the Canada Council, the Ontario Arts Council, and the Government of Canada through the Book Publishing Industry Development Program. Canadä

DISTRIBUTION

CANADA: General Distribution Services, 325 Humber College Blvd., Toronto, ON M9W 7C3

ECW PRESS
ecwpress.com

Acknowledgements

Thank you immeasurably to the following people and places for encouragement, support, and assorted inspiration:

Greg Attwell, Barbara Baskier, Shelley & Tom Bernard, Peter Darbyshire, The I.V. Lounge, Dave Johnny, Terri-Lynn Lawrence, Alexandra Leggat, Suzy Lovegrove, Stephanie Morley, The Rhino, Stuart Ross, Shelagh M. Rowan-Legg, Kate Sutherland, and Paul Vermeersch.

Thanks to Michael Holmes, one kick ass editor, and the ECW gang.

Also thanks to the Toronto Arts Council and the Ontario Arts Council for support during the writing of this book.

Some poems have appeared, in some version or other, in the following publications: *Fashion Tips for the Female Pirate* (wayward armadillo press), *The Fiddlehead, Kitten Skulls and Chicken Bones* (wayward armadillo press), *The Lazy Writer, Queen Street Quarterly, sub-*TERRAIN, *Vintage '97-98, Word, Zygote,* and on *Definitely Not the Opera* (CBC Radio 1).

Contents

Four:

one

Drain, drain the bowl, each fearless soul —
Let the world wag as it will. Let the heavens
growl, the devil howl —

Anne Bonny, 1700-1722

"Dead Dog," I lectured myself, "you're stupid because you gnaw at, and then throw away, everyone whom you most love. You're dead and you've got to live. It's living dogs who can search for treasure."

Kathy Acker, *Pussy, King of the Pirates*

Songs to Drown By

Whenever a woman whistles,
somewhere there is a sailor
who drowns.

Pursed lips, a stolen pair
of black sunglasses,
I don't give a damn
about my bad reputation.

The music rumbles off-shore
storms and they roll in,
throw up their skirts,
click heels like leprechaun
chorus girls. Fling sailboats
up against cliffs.

Bottles and planks,
confetti. Shower a choir
of harpies, feathers
razor-tipped, they erupt
into wingspan. Slice open
the air, pitch fatal songs
through the smiling
faces of daughters.

Sometimes desperate
captains buy the wind
from witches on the piers
of Scotland.

They shiver, snatch it

from outstretched palms,
its brine curls
their tongues. They stroll back
to smug ships, cheeks puffed,
whistling ballads, while ancient purses
bulge and burst on shore.

With a Carving Knife

Meanwhile, your birth rattles the town,
averted eyes — you're stashed
with the servants' gossip.
Tongues flickering: *the lawyer's*
bastard girl got some temper.

You steal kitchen knives and duel
stable boys. Nick their pocked cheeks
and laugh, thirteen years old, a glaring head
taller, illegitimate daughter.

Daddy creeps down midnight
hallways to the maid's room, until
one night he peels back her quilt
and finds instead his clever wife.

The kitchen girl, mouse eyes beading —
Nobody wants you here, anyway,
pink face bloated with smirks —
You're a disgrace.

A hot palm splits her
lips; you warned her
didn't you? But still she squeaks,
Your daddy doesn't want you
loud and ugly as a boy.

Half the morning spent shining
that carving knife you slide
from your skirts, her belly
spreads into bright sunbursts

and your red hair laced tight
with spiders, sugar and spice,
Irish eyelashes edged in ice.

Fashion Tips for the Female Pirate

At sixteen you teach yourself the rigour
     and delicacy
  of breast binding. The sash
torn wide
     from the starched apron of the lady
  whose dishes you scrub.
 How tight to tie the fabric
         and still breathe.

How to piss over the edge of a ship
     through a hollow gourd —
  which type straps on best,
way before packin' was just another party trick.

    The 1700s: tar was still
  the preservative
     for captured pirate skin.
  Suspended along the waterfront,
     hoops and chains
       dangling iron cages.

Thick night of tides and rust,
  the town waving torches and songs,
tossing broken bottles
  between bars —

the tar only cracking
     as the flesh begins to bloat.

Wedding Present

. . . a smile,
after all, is two sneers on the same lip.
  — Simon Armitage

Carolina tavern, *The Salty Dog,* dirt-packed
doorway, coastal earthworms squirm
up for storms, blind to stumbling
heels, clattering bottles.

Night when the sky bursts and the sea
reaches up with a rumbling cheer, James Bonny
tosses Anne a drunken dare —
one green eye, one brown flicker over her
damp dress, hovering in folds as she
shakes mud from her hair. The bar maid
asks her age, where her father is.

Anne spits, grinds
contempt beneath her boots and laughter.
Her prize, all the whiskey she can gulp
on the stool rattling next to James.
Other men pound their glasses,
and she bares her teeth to the challenge.

James' cold sailor fingers pluck
at mismatched brass buttons, trying to recall
each of the corpses he tore them from.
Can't, but knows how many wide
acres stretch across Anne's father's plantation.

Anne claps her hands in the doorway,
the room sways to watch, her head

tossed back, cheeks hot she dangles
the thickest earthworm
high and drops it. Her throat a tunnel
caving in, arms and lips
wide, eyes never leaving his.

She laughs, swallows three
more in case anyone missed the first,
leans across James to the barmaid,
cup tilted, demanding her reward.

Keep your distance, she says to Anne,
I don't like your kind. Pushes back the empty glass.
Anne lifts it in a feline arch, snaps
her arm and there is glass
tumbling festive
around tapping feet.

The barmaid tries to toss her
to the storm,
instead loses two
front teeth in the scuffle,
split from her jaw,
rattling Anne's skirts.

The night Anne marries James Bonny
she gives him a necklace, both talisman
and warning, two teeth
strung up, dangling.

Keelhauling

The flogging does not break
me. Secrets I arch into —
I wear these stripes
with a haughtiness, an expensive
fashion not so easily afforded
by other shivering captives.

I am being tried for impetuousness;
things have been worse. They caught me
edging from the captain's cabin,
she smoothed the ineffable lines
of my back, my shoulders, with an oil
stolen from royalty. Nothing to do
with pity, or with also
dressing as a man.

But this crew is restless,
Jack tears a mean streak,
Pierre composes torments like arias.
They stoke even the barnacles,
everyone's eyes
narrow, fists curl.

Anne sleeps the sure night of one
who instills fear, loose cannonballs
rumble toward me, I scuttle
the deck. The crew loops a rope
around the ship's widest bulge,
drags it along the rough arms of waiting
starfish.

Disdain reddens my blood.
I know well I killed
my own husband and took
his clothes to be out here.

They twist my hands
fast behind my back,
Pierre holds the left and Jack
the right ankle as they link
thirty pound cannonballs to my feet,
slap my face when I smile
and whistle at gulls.

Sharp fingers of rope scrape
the scabs I ignore,
and still I say nothing. These men know
little of how a hand fits the cutlass;
that I could teach them
roots their fear, and for now
they hate me.

The side tackle is hitched hard to the mainyard,
half the leering crew waits portside
dangling the rope's end like a sneer,
before they plunge me through
and under.

They tried this torture once
and drowned a man who
sliced off his own index finger
for a larger share of silver.
His bloodied body
a vengeance of barnacles.

I sear through the water,
tossed against the keel,
a fissure scrawls to the bone and
pulls the sea into my shoulder.

They wrench the rope, a blue starfish
gouges a spiny arm through my cheek,
my face in flames.

The cheers rouse Anne — she
shoots two men who answer
too slowly. Her red hair
sprawls flag-like, a welcome
as I sputter back on deck.

And it is my survival that kills
the lieutenant, puts me
in his place, as Anne also knows
it takes less courage to torture
than to survive.

The Carpenter

Hands tuned to silence
leaks dry, turn branch
to plank. His saw valued
more than Anne's sword:
ship's most vital crew member,
he is also the surgeon.

Two months fevered, gone.
The bullet torn through
Pierre's leg, the flesh
swelling to yellow, then black.
Blisters bubble
like a stew, the stench
deters company.

He is drunk, it is merciful.
Two new crewmen hold down
a shoulder, the sea holds
its breath and the moon
is enough to see by.

The carpenter smoothes splinters
and a generous shot of rum,
raises the saw; the crew
tightens their arms, their
eyelids, Calico Jack
turns away, drinks fast
over his lover's screams.

Pierre is relieved
of his rotten leg, a hair

above the knee.

Gulls pluck
the bone clean, boiled water
rinses the saw;
the carpenter turns tool to
instrument. Draws

strings over blade,
coaxes music in heatwaves.
Songs to soothe the blood;
metal sighs
from jagged teeth

dissolving rust
to silver refrain,
from hands that tame
the cutting edge
of pull and sever.

Masquerade

They sail without borders,
shatter stars that mimic
themselves on water.

Anne plucks a turtle
and gores it, drags
the blood across her cheek
with the calluses that scale
her *red right hand*.

They open the night,
loot a merchant vessel
brimming with dresses, purple
silk and bodices spilling
out portals toward a London
bordello. That was Pierre's idea.

Pierre the Pansy, resident dressmaker,
stitched Calico Jack's name — his pants'
patchwork velvet — everyone's
outfit, for comfort and style in months
of death and not washing.

Salt teases the air, pirate's
confetti. Anne and Mary,
Pierre and Jack pull satin
tight across hipbones. Skirts bluster
over hot thighs. They dip their palms
in reptilian blood, smear along
rough faces and arms hardened
by brine and yoking the wind.

Fingers laced and dripping
they lurch across the deck,
the sky sways and bends
to their first Atlantic
triumph, they stomp
their feet in time with
the waves' splash against
boots, the mist's rise entwined
in matted hair.

Looming along the edge of morning,
another ship. Bigger this
time, heavy with gold coins
and spices, rare feathers
and well-oiled pistols.

Anne's crew scurries to shed silk
puckers and ruffled tatters, cock
the cannons and aim, but she holds
course, spits down her commands:
Keep dancing, pass between you
the shell of this turtle, and smile
wider than this grappling hook.

And so the second ship sees
four garish whores, bleeding
a waltz against morning, flailing
cutlasses and corpses' grins
against a man, swallowed in burlap,
dangling high from the mast.

They pull back their breath, their
cannons' angle, and surrender,

to this unflinching ship full of men
made of sackcloth and stained rags,
the theatrics of dead, laughing whores.

Under Current

Your complicity is weighted
with heavy stones, bound
in meaty tendons,
and dropped.

I try to count the ripples
on the river,
calculate in years
how old the water is;

how long it takes
for meaning to resurface
and dissolve.

What are these blotches, these
Rorschach spills
seeping memory along my limbs —

This week presses my face
like a father's hands.

I am a diver, a pirate,
an imposter. This green
leans too much against me,
fool's gold doubloons
in every vowel.

Whose skin is this I wear
stretched tight around me
like a name; the bruised
balloon body of a drowned woman?

My hair tangles and drapes
into plaits of seaweed,
eyes scale over to
gills, blink oxygen
instead of light.

Netted, I am hauled up
and dragged to a jagged shore.
Split and rinsed —

I am pure.
Catch of the day,
I offer myself up

to those with mesh
beneath their tongues,
barbs dangling from teeth.

You devour all in searing shreds,
juices burning rivers
through your chin

until these men
with salt-chapped hands
are full and drowsing,

and one by one
topple and hiss
like flaming towers
into the sea.

How to Sink a Ship

He unlaces my girdle
of strict, severed hands,
teasing away stiff finger
bones, drops
them into a pile next
to the green candles sprawling
an arc around my bed, a hot
horseshoe. I tell him
he is *good luck,*

that I can sink ships
by building wax models
and throwing them into the sea.

His patient smile unhinges
my intent, I layer
a raft and pitch it offshore
with six dozen tulips
everyday, petals
like cannonballs
trail the surface.

The rest I tuck
beneath his eyelids
and wait for morning.

The Piracy of Breathing

Your voice is a dangerous
ink, thick and sticky
as the breath trapped between us
and words, seeping
through me, indigo and viral,
bursting veins and staining
my terrified hands.

I am growing terrible violets
over my skin, an armour
of petals dusted with a bitter powder
to repel your hot tongue, purple
flecks, tiny, but more deadly
than love, in the same
languid dissolve.

I want to dress for you
in skirts of fire,
with the splintered bones
of pirates rattling
'round my neck. I raise
to you this flawless cutlass:
Mary in her vicious boots,
I will grind my black heel
into your twisting throat

and pluck out
your fist-sized heart.

You don't see these costumes,
the Jolly Roger fluttering beneath

my black-painted eyelids.

Instead, you dress me in absences,
ropes and stripes of leather,
delicacies you leave coiled about
my limbs as snakes and charm bracelets.

That is how I was taught
to love — the sharp stinging
memory welts, and the
ships' white sails
ruffling the wind.

two

She stands before him clothed in garments of flaming fire, inspiring terror and making body and soul tremble, full of frightening eyes, in her hand a sword dripping bitter drops.

Barbara Black Koltuv, *The Book of Lilith*

the comrade/ twin whose palm would bear a lifeline like our own:

decisive, arrowy, forked lightning of insatiate desire

Adrienne Rich, *"Natural Resources"*

How to Juggle

I level my eyes,
cup my palms
and hover, remorseless,
a supplicant.

I incite the air to violence,
wring cyclones from quiet,
until all the voyeurs shiver
and scuttle home, tuck
themselves into their televisions.

Hands quicker than the frog's
tongue, quicker than jealousy,
I pluck five smiling infants

from their cribs
and toss them,
like red rubber balls,
spinning, until only a juggler
can tell them apart.

Naming Judith

What a beautiful, challenging body she had!
With a terrible beginning of consciousness, like a
splendid she-animal, nearly grown.
 — Martha Ostenso, *Wild Geese*

Dig my name from the earth.
Align the rusted
iron letters into an equation,
a riddle, your swaying gypsy
skirts and hot chains, alive
alive.

Judith's breasts pulse against
the dirt. She knows the
secret in the sum
of my name, hears the flight
of her voice

as it lifts her, rung by
halo, above the tyrannical smoke
of Caleb's flesh. These fields of flax
we ignite, he flails
at the centre, in burning
scarecrow terror.

I am the owl, my name
the molten screech —
it pours from me
and the ground trembles.

Our shrieks
of fleshy hunger

drown out
midnight prayers.

I hold the ladder and Judith
climbs, wearing purple
lace and clove oil, boots
heavy, scuffed with ciphers.

A red silk scarf
tied around her waist
dangles bells, prophecies,
the still-warm head
of Nebuchadnezzar.

The Immortality Beads

they keep calling me . . .
      — Joy Division

I flutter and hum at the bedpost,
a famished mosquito, a dragonfly
with opal wings and too many eyes.

I claim your nameless children
as my own, before you feel their
claustrophobic lurch

against your womb; before your
stuck and grunting lover's
climax, they are mine.

The bedroom thickens with
skin and candlesmoke —
I rest my feet on the flame,

slip silent into your desire
align my hungry pulse
with yours. Fingertips sear and clutch

your lover's frantic spine,
veins spark like vicious clouds,
teeth grind to diamonds.

You shudder and drift,
rustle like furtive questions,
weary crickets.

This is when I curl

into your blood, the singe
of scandal, unseen

but irrevocable, I
toss back my head
and from my own acidic

menses, leave you
one glittering drop, heavy
with enough poison

for an entire town.

Nightmare Troubadour

I exist in the threshold
between events, the red space
within what could have been.

I lurk in heavy stone arches,
am most accustomed to doorways —
the tollkeeper of entrances and exits.

I am suspense, the thick hot plane
when you hold your breath; it prickles,
bubbles up through the pores on your chest.

My flight is noiseless, a screech
owl, I land with clawed feet on the rafters
of your sleep.

Children, I visit each of you,
a satellite dancer,
black moon invisible from the Earth,
invisible even when close enough
to touch.

I slip between your lips when you inhale,
when you fall from the edges of thought
this aperture is mine.

Now you know where
nightmares come from:
I can turn my horned and flaming
insect head all the way around.

I see every fear
at once and one by one
I hold them in my feathery hands,
these precious trinkets

of air and fire,
barren soil and the night wind,
the inscrutable logic of unknown
languages — the stuff
I am made of.

From this no amulet can protect you
no cold and graceful metal
thrown against my teeth
will bar me, no charcoal
inscriptions of the names of angels.

Try to elude the monstrous
jaws of ravaged dogs,
the hard grey dentist with
tentacle hands.

Try to run, and the air
thickens with resistance.
Fall to the ground, and
cannot climb to your feet.

You know, now,
who shoves you down,
and holds you there.

three

The tulips are too red in the first place, they hurt me.
Even through the gift paper I could hear them breathe
Lightly, through their white swaddlings, like an awful baby.

Sylvia Plath, *"Tulips"*

Sarah

She is not
a noun, like *sister*, or
any part of speech.

She only exists
in this poem, or as
a birth
prior to mine.

Hers is an empty name;
an ellipsis.

You should know, now,
there was no such thing
as date rape, we didn't
call it anything, then.

Twenty-one is old enough
for a mother to teach
a daughter about words:
Mother, daughter, sister.

There is a hollow space
beneath *sister*;
her name is all of her
I know.

Caesarean

The baby dies before his mother
wakes. They shuffle him off
to a cool sour room,
waiting for her anaesthetic
to leak away.

Blinds pulled hard against
the town, leaves like gossip
rattle hospital panes,
shotgun shells loose
in the trunk.

They split her gut wide,
tear the baby from her
when they will not separate.

He kicks without sound
at an hour pressed hard
on his chest, the air
too heavy to navigate.

Her mouth, her lungs still
jammed with feathers
thick as chloroform
and burst pillows —

propping the still head in his hand
the doctor thrusts him
toward her, almost
apologizing for the silence.

You'll want to hold him,
he insists as she pushes
him away, twists the paper
dress into fists.

They always
want to hold them,
anyway.

She clenches her eyes shut
until the nurses shrug
and the father slips home
to finish packing the car
for his hunting trip.

His Chevy lurches down
exit ramps, towns slur
further behind, his knuckles white
and snapping as rocks
edge closer to the road

and trees grow taller,
lean in like accusations.

Imitation Wood

The gun rack: smoothed over
with green felt, plastic wood —
upturned claws,
clinging, empty,
to the panelled wall.

Winter coats dangle
like deer carcasses,
or moose.

Christmas tinsel
chokes synthetic pine.
Five years old, I want

to peel open a ribbon-bound box
but Mom smiles no, squints
through the window, waits.

Father sways into a hot whiskey grin,
leaning, father of doorways,
squirms out of his red lumber jacket,
tosses it toward the gun rack.

Kitchen voices fight through
the howl of kettles, the rattle
of spoons.

His jacket slumps to the carpet;
I will hang it up for you:

on tip-toes,
can't reach (lazy)
even if I'm really quiet (stupid).

I untie the box.
a tiny china tea set:
blue flowers layer and
smother white porcelain.

Tea, Daddy?

And we are taut as strings,
our tendons twang as we tip
the cups, and slurp the air.

Faultlines

She was ten, her arm laced with glass
from the back door, seeping over skin
a sudden latticework of red.

It wasn't the punching through, but
the pulling back in that opened
her, from wrist to shoulder,
in a network of lines that intersect.

Doors slam against the afternoon,
a crunch of tires roll
my eyes and nothing is out of place
here but the quiet; the air
stilling over me.

Three hundred and fifty-six stitches to hold
her together, a lurching
tightrope walker: sister
of edges.

A decade later, she says, *Someone*
is being mean to Bunny, a man
writes me stories and poems, one
every day and always
he kills me at the end.

This family mapped in white
sprawled across her forearm,
grafting memory onto skin.

I trawl my longest nail along, here,
and here, I trace this one:
our willow tree, branches
that cut into palms but still
it was close enough to flying.

And this one, my cold finger drags, this one
is the jagged feather earring torn
clean from my lobe, *Who
do you think you are, anyway?*

And this one, the arc clawed
into the yard at the end of my dog's
rattling chain, or the unnamed road
Dad left him on.

I want to peel it back, she says,
open the scars and there will be
Mother's shrieks swerving
across town, the tree, that
ruptured house.

I want my arm back, what is still
under the jigsaw puzzle of skin.
Write me something mean, and secret, she says,
to send back.

Luna Moth

Each breath is a school bus dropping
over the icy edge of your vision.
The driver left to freeze
on the side of the highway

curled tight around the kitchen
knife you clutched
in your jacket like a passport.

It takes four cops and a husband
to unravel you
into the car.

Sirens spin a blue and red
web of light to net you blind,
pin you to the psych-ward bulletin board.

The days splinter, and carve
caverns along the borders
of memory.

Your hands shake:
too jagged to even smoke,
or touch the turned backs
of a roomful of daughters.

Upstairs*

He kicks, splashes
without interruption
in the patented suction-cup
bath seat, warm water
playground all to himself

while they watched
TV downstairs.

He leans closer —
seven months of Damian —
reaches into himself
reflected in
twenty-three centimetres
of bath water,
snapping suction.

They frequently pressed
the mute button
so they could listen.

The water takes his hands
breaks his fall
and holds him, until
streams pour down
the television screen.

*Toronto Star, Oct. 19, 1995

49

Prodigal

Maybe there's a town you've never heard of,
a house reeling on the outskirts.
Someone else's family at Christmas.
Ribbons, papercuts, fingers split open

like secrets. Guests, small talk, *those goddamned immigrants*
taking over, taking the Lord's prayer away from our kids.
Heads swoon agreement, cups rattle, a daughter
slips downstairs to kids, blazing cars, Nintendo.

Maybe the father won't carve the turkey,
won't leave the bedroom, the Absolut, for two days —
and they eat without him.

The night before, visiting friends,
the photo album of OPP doubles, a book full
of hanging teens in *Just Do It* t-shirts,

naked, punctured wives, Southern Ontario
beaches awash with splintered ribcages,
guys in rec rooms with faces blown half off,
blood still sticky in the photo lab.

And he is slumped, alive, sputtering
to rooms full of relatives: *divorce, divorce.*
Maybe she finds her mother

at the kitchen sink on Boxing Day
pouring out bottles, *Any of this yours?*
And they giggle like schoolgirls, *No,*
but I'll take it anyway.

Girl Refuses to Do Up Coat

Sixth grade, your father opens
your nose like a tap, family
car idling in the driveway
rough with chestnuts you chuck
at the neighbours' dirty, unfed cats.

Doesn't even turn around, does he,
navigates the swing through the rearview.
His shouts rattle the windows, a hot flash
on your face, your bulky Bi-Way coat
stippled with stains. Dots to connect
in snow, trail of breadcrumbs home.

But you had some tricks yourself,
could turn the sky to steel
with an upward glance,
a smirk, the screech and clang
as you drew the blinds

tight over the world, finished it.
Woke to a sweat cold as hands.
You didn't want to die, did you?
Not yet, not really, and not in that town.

He must have grown remorse
like mold over God-fearing hands,
though they pinned you at the wrists
when you fought back
with nails, spit, insults.

Later, you'd hunt weakness in others,
fear that plucks out eyes like birds,
lovers that pin your hands above your head
at the wrists. A wedding — you throw
birdseed instead of rice.

It seems more humane, really,
until someone mentions Hitchcock.

Reruns

Nights when you have to ask yourself
Could I be wrong? and know that you are.
This time terribly. All the tough-guy cranked up
Die, Die My Darling can't stifle
the high-pitched whine in your own head.
Just piss off the neighbours and the roaches
and realize: romance is another product
you can no longer afford.

There's bad credit under your fingernails.
R9s at the banks, at the malls, even your social
transactions decline. Nobody gives a damn
about trust anymore. It's Frosh Week reruns,
vodka and humiliation, best friend
fucking your boyfriend down the hall, and you —
the last to know.

No. That was years ago. Today was a pathology
of optimism. Household cleansers, pink plastic
razors, clean sheets, and no drinks before seven:
He'll remember sloppy.

But the evening is all dialtones,
and your patience grows so thin
it cuts; while your plans, your kitchen,
your schoolgirl fantasies clatter
in a ruin of bottles.

Then your father calls from Mexico.
He is attending parties and picnics.
Is keeping a diary. He seems pleased.

The weather is warm, though storms
crawl in from the mountains.
A woman from Guadalajara

stood him up today. *Good,* you tell him,
You're a bastard. He hangs up,
doesn't call back. It will be another
two years, and you'll hate yourself
for recognizing his voice.

Dollmaker

Molly, she never gets out.
No one knows where she leaves off
and the rocking chair starts, fingernails
clawed deep in tiny armrests.

There were rooms thick with choking,
walls bursting open like storms,
a sky on fire. Jim tears her
from the doorway, hair tailing
a comet. The youngest girl, lost
in that fire. Molly's pink
floral dress, this is permanent.

And Cora, she's a whore.
Just look at those boots.
Real leather, and eyeliner
out to here. Listen. She'll tell you
the day you'll die, and where
he spent last night. Tells fortunes
from the bottom of a gin glass:
that's handblown.

Verna, she's the fanatic.
Left her dirty husband
vomiting in the sink. Mails
her pension cheques
to Jesus. That's prime time.
Read the fine print, two pages
of Leviticus, by hand.

Burnt mohair, chisel and armature.
Two months apiece, during Oprah
and Swaggart. A contest
in Indiana, statewide. Her daughter
says *My favorites are the Supremes.
Those dresses!* And Mama can hear

the backup singers, all doo-wop
and sway. Row house on Maple,
emptied rooms, husband
vomiting. Gin and juice, so many
other men. That fire.

Crafts Today, she slams
a clipping to the fridge. First
place is Mimi, all Styrofoam and silk and
cheap costume jewelry. Looks peaked
and itchy. Get out the clay,
the thin brushes. Maybe
she'll win next year.

Bad Association

When I was ten my great-grandma wasn't talking
to my grandma because she wasn't talking to my
aunt who we weren't allowed
to talk to because she got

disfellowshipped for divorcing
my uncle, a truck driver
who used to come into the house to
get money for the hookers
waiting in the truck in the driveway.

At the meetings the elders would tell us
that people who aren't Jehovah's Witnesses
are bad association —
because they do things that are pagan
like celebrate Christmas and birthdays.

In the Bible, the only birthday party
is when John the Baptist
gets his head cut off.

Relativity

With my tongue I polish all the watermarks
from the precious silver I never owned.
Leave it in my will to my father, he can use it
to fix his car
or blackmail himself.
There is still time
to re-think small engine repair,
disowning the concept of family.

four

It was as though they could both smell tumult coming, it was as though Cat stank of something that was either cataclysm or omnipotence and they knew it.

Janette Turner Hospital, *The Last Magician*

Sabrina

Wore hot plastic colours
high heels
& a peacock feather grin.
Brought cleavage to librarian
& taught me more than the Dewey decimal system.

At fourteen I didn't know the difference
between a penis
that was circumcised
and one that wasn't.

In green crayon
she cartooned me
a before & after.

We hid it
in the bottom of the garbage can
to avoid scaring the little kids
or the head librarian.

Mom didn't want me
to visit her
after she moved away,

I modeled a turquoise bikini
for her & she let me
drink Southern Comfort, laughing
while we tangoed across the beach
that was her living room.

Tripping over each other
we dipped and swerved
that night until
I fell asleep
in hot pink.

The Better To

for *The Kickin' Vixen*

Skin alive a whistle
                    flayed wide
          curbside howls
                    scratched in concrete.
    Broken bottle raised
          head-on come-on
                    can't keep
keeping eyes down, hands
                    down, pockets stuffed.
          My what big —
                    steps to swerve by
      day in or night
out, haunches wound
                    to pounce, street lights
          rattle, fireflies in jars
                    screwed tight.
Bet she is, and
          My what big —
      teeth glint, slack jaw
                    splinter and a swift
          kick peels back
                    sheep's clothing she
      circles blood scents
          eyes moon yellow,
switchblade hackles
                    raised throbbing
      they are seven —
                    The better to turn
                    inside   out done.

The Monochrome Man

I was killing myself only
but it was always the bystander who died.
    — Dennis Nilsen

        Don Juan to dead men,
you dust yourself with a cool sheen
        of white powder before
    strangling your lovers,
  slowing your own breath
            your heart, but no —

    the organs
are always a problem. Bursting your chest,
      they clutter the plumbing
    as you try to flush away
      the flesh.

Each morning you peel back your London
        floorboards, gather a man in your arms
    and bathe him, gently
dress him in a double-breasted suit, ruffle
      the newspaper, rearrange
    the assorted heads set evenly along the mantle.

But mostly, you prop
      each man up in an armchair, the TV haze
    making the living room so normal.
And you at the centre,
      social butterfly, making all the small talk
    never again alone, and writing
  each of them
      delicate sonnets.

The Worst-Ever Decomp

He's the Molly Maid of homicide,
suicide, meth labs. Gazes at America
through plexi-glass goggles,
the doorway of a Motel 6,
the Stop 'n' Shop. He mops up
murders that pelt the landscape
like hail, Bible-style.

He chokes back no nine to five,
sweats no three piece. Knight
in a Tyvex suit, flailing hoses
like tentacles. Wears a respirator
for a face.

Cut his teeth in an upscale condo
in Oakland, a dead husband
full of more holes than cops'
notions. Reams of maggots
squirming like a teenage acid trip.
The wife: nowhere.
Pot of coffee burnt thick
on the stove.

No friends to notice the guy's absence,
his hide-a-bed a cauldron of juices,
until neighbours complain about the smell.
Emmylou left on repeat:
I was ready for love
I was ready for the money . . .

Cops take a locked box
of homemade videos — giddy threesomes
scrambling on satin sheets,
men in masks and hoods, bull whips
hungry as lizard tongues.

That there's some fucked up shit,
the cops laugh, elbow each other,
gag and hit the road. No amount
of coffee can cover the smells.
Later, they ask their wives,
please, to tie them up.

But the crime scene cleaner knows
you got to be careful with the body.
Use an extractor. There's an enzyme
to neutralize that spilled cranial fluid,
that blood. Hepatitis can dry up
in expensive carpeting, become airborne.
Get sucked into the lungs during dinner parties.
Land in lawsuits from new homeowners.

He wanted to call his company
Aftermath, the glamour, all very
Keitel, but he worried about credibility.
Settled more to the point:
Crime Scene Cleaners. He wants
to be bodyguard-rich, buying
helicopters and divorces like
candy. He loves his job,
It's my girl, my dope.

Fly Away Home

Her cousin Kenny is older, maybe ten.
Snakes oozing out of pockets,
he raises the roof with the cock of an eyebrow.

Kim's mom knows he's trouble
But he's family, and *Who else
is there for her to play with?*
Besides Johnny next door — but
Everybody knows he's slow.

Summer grass quivers shoulder-high, sharp
as a porcupine's back, claws roadmaps
across their arms and the August sun
scorches any hope of rain.

A door gapes, an unhinged jaw.
The barn abandoned before these three
were born, and they squirm through,
Johnny in the middle, they are always careful
not to lose him.

Nestled in stale hay,
a litter of kitten skulls.
Kenny throws one at Kim
who throws it at Johnny,
and the afternoon lunges
into a game of catch

until Johnny catches one too hard
and it crumbles in his hand.
Kenny distracts from the crying,

promises to show them both
the latest secret he stole

from his dad but first
they must swear
on one of the two remaining
kittens not to tell.

You hold it like this
he scissors the cigarette
between his first two fingers,
singes it lit on the third try.

They all cough and Kim knows
it's not as much fun as the kitten skulls,
but Kenny is a year older
so she squints *Like this?*
and they have to light
a whole new one
when she flicks too hard.

Heads buzzing, carried off
by bees, their eyes sting and stomachs lurch.
Kim laughs when Kenny throws up,
wipes his mouth with a fistful of hay
and bursts into shouts
C'mon! Let's get outta here!

The hay catches first, billows,
fills the barn and pushes Kenny and Kim out,
Johnny in tow, but he shakes free,
goes back for the kitten skulls.

They try to scream him out,
he can't see to find the kittens
so he stands still, just staring
into flame. He's never seen anything so big
and beautiful really, the way everything
becomes part of it.

The Longest Covered Bridge in the World

Before cars
young couples would clop-clop
into the middle of the bridge,
stretching a road through
low-hanging sky
tug the horse to a pause,

the wood absorbing breath charged
with fumbling hands, lips, blood pressure.

The horses meanwhile
avert their eyes,
memorize the angles of ceiling beams,
the soft meandering
grains of wood, daydreaming
the things horses
envision: fields, legs leaping fences,
other horses.

The fathers of the town
drove their families to church
but scratched their beards,
snapped the reins,
as every Sunday
the horses stopped
in the centre of the bridge, patiently.

New York City Poem #4

Your fingernails etched a map
from my scalp to my feet.

This time I am the one
flayed, peeling back
the skin to navigate,

gouging into the streets
of New York City.

Your black leather jacket
hangs your absence
in my hall closet, I take
the shadow hostage but

you chew straight through
the strings and weave
circles around me —
a mockery, a memory net.
Elusive marionette
you spin off.

A quarter century
running marathons of departure,
false starts, you avoid
finish lines —
could slice you clean in two.

New York City Poem #6

Drunk in a Spanish bar in Soho,
I've walked nine hours now
trying to lose your
absence as easily
as you shed my skin.

Reptilian Houdini,
a tilt of the head
a rippling spine
you twist into another
rice paper costume change,

a new layer of detachment.
It's the epidermal equinox,

whatever season or touch
you choose to ignore.

Mary Tyler Morphine

the Gasoline Queen of Tottenham

She rakes the green
of golf courses with
an iron manicure,
Bridget Jones with no
diary, just tonic

terrorism and gin. Playing
for keeps and no collar,
triceps so tight
they serenade, as you
fumble a bill for the fill-up

flip to page three,
Sunshine Girl, your second finger
pared down to the first
knuckle, a stub, same
as every third man in town.

An industrial recall
in the '70s, no one
asks any questions. After

midnight she slides one hand slowly
along the cool red bulge
of a '67 fender, peels
out, never stops for you —
hood up, and pacing by the course.

Jackrabbit

I don't know what he wants from me.
Pockets full of dice, a mouth full of diamonds.
A puff of smoke, the brim of a top hat.

We talk too much, auctioneers,
throw down stories like careless
hands of poker. I say many
inane things, what I think

passes for wit, incantations.
Sweet tiny bells chiming in chorus
whenever I open my mouth
I eat guardian angels . . . .

By now, he has quit certain things: cocaine,
caffeine, nicotine. Coercions by teachers, orderlies.
I tell him I too know about small
Ontario towns. I paint my nails

slut red, consider buying a cellular phone.
He is an aging punk, prefers
pretty blonde actresses who are cruel.

He is generous, thorough, confessional.
Prefers to fuck me from behind,
and though tattoos don't bother me,

I am relieved.
We are both frantic to be loved,
though not by each other.

There is a jackrabbit springing
across his chest, ears flat,
claws poised.

Chicken Bones and Charcoal Sticks

You sleep brittle with chicken bones and charcoal sticks,
share this bed with all the dead birds
whose nests you plagiarize, shredded paper
surrounding you, as though you want to trap
yourself in my words, as though
either of us could live like this.

You're not as fragile as you think you are;
I know you didn't snap
any of those feathered necks
yourself. It's all just tapeloops
and backward masking, take-out
wings and old Talking Heads albums —
It's not so cool to have so many problems.

Took three years for your letter
to arrive, all dissonance and fractured
black ink, conservatory paper, listing
how many minutes it took to make
her come, while I waited up for you
in that rattling house.

Summer became Greyhound bathrooms
and forgotten area codes, arbitrary rail transfers,
Saskatoon train station at three a.m.
The inventory of bizarre murders in prairie
suburbs. Cab driver slurs: *You're stayin' in a bad
neighbourhood missy, one of 'em found just back there.*

Limbs in railyards, tufts of hair clumped along
pipelines. I smile and tip him more than I should,

still racing my arteries with Via Rail and
cheap Winnipeg speed, knowing finally
how wide the Saskatchewan sky can be
when you're angry and in love
with a fire-eater. Or maybe
just the fire.